Where's My Monster?

By Wendy Monica Winter
Illustrated by Yulia Popova

Copyright © 2022 Wendy Monica Winter
Illustrations and Graphic Designs by Yulia Popova (popova_y_n@mail.ru)

All rights reserved. No part of this book may be reproduced in any matter without the express written consent of the author, except in the case of brief excerpts in critical reviews and articles. All inquiries should be addressed to Wendy Monica Winter at wendymonicawinter@gmail.com.

Published by Wendy Monica Winter
Hardcover ISBN 978-1-990486-06-7
Paperback ISBN 978-1-990486-04-3
eBook ISBN 978-1-990486-05-0
Squamish, British Columbia, Canada
V20220324

ISBN Published Heritage Branch Library and Archives Canada

For my mother, Trudy, whose selfless giving and care has been a continual light in my life.
WENDY MONICA WINTER

For my children, Vika and Andrey, may the light of kindness and love always illuminate your life.
YULIA POPOVA

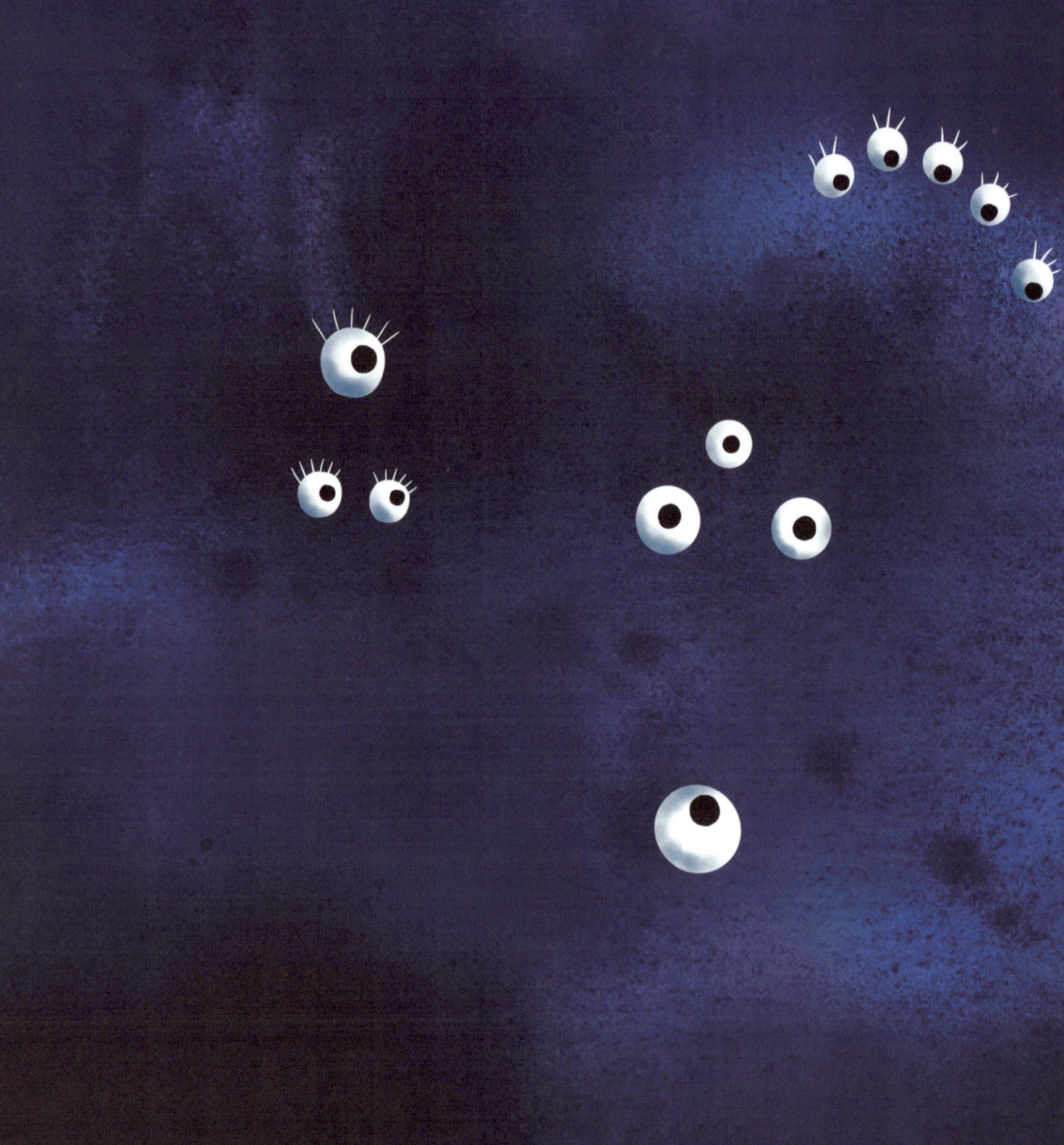

I'm HUNGRY!

Don't worry. We will get a nice meal very soon.

I hear something!

I'm not going in there.

Monsters are scary!

Why are those kids afraid?

If you bring a light into a dark room, it lights up the room. Bring darkness into a lit room and it does nothing.

I will use my LIGHT.

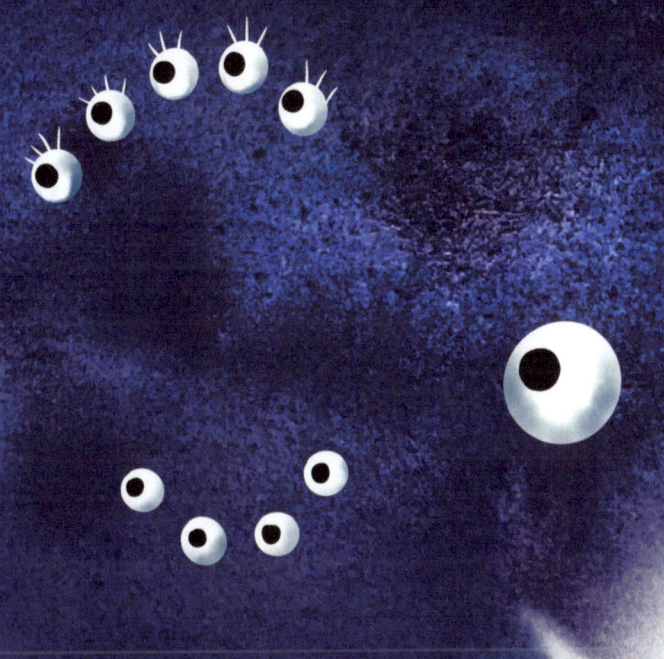

More FEAR!
Yummy!

I find the LIGHT comforting and warm.

Hello there! Aren't you cute!

I don't feel hungry anymore.

It does feel nice to be warm, and I do feel full.

Me too!

Me three!

Me four!

Me five!

Wow! A whole bunch of not-so-scary scary monsters.

What is your name?

Your LIGHT is beautiful.

Look at what LIGHT can do.

Shall I show you where there is some more LIGHT?

Where's my MONSTER?

Darkness cannot drive out darknness;
only LIGHT can do that.
Hate cannot drive out hate;
only LOVE can do that.

Martin Luther King Jr.

For more quotes on light and dark, please visit
wendymonicawinter.com/light

Can you find these items in the Story?

Crystal with rainbow

Scary monster drawing

Seed of Life

Chalice with roses

White Rabbit

Dark Star

Golden Sun

Lighthouse Calendar

How many eyeballs are in this book?
To check your answer, please visit wendymonicawinter.com

Where's My Monster? Questions

In your opinion, what is Lucy's superpower?

For the creators of this book, the LIGHT that Lucy holds represents the inner LIGHT of the soul of this small and brave girl. The warm LIGHT reflects the beauty of her kind heart. What does the LIGHT represent to you?

What FEARS have you overcome? How did they become not-so-scary?

What FEARS are you still facing?
What LIGHT can you shine on them so that they don't have power over you?

FOR MORE FUN,

CHECK OUT THE FIRST BOOK IN THE *WHERE'S MY?* SERIES

Goodreads Choice Awards Nominee 2021 Nominee ***** Pinnacle Book Achievement Award Gold
Book Excellence Award Gold ***** Literary Titan Book Award Gold

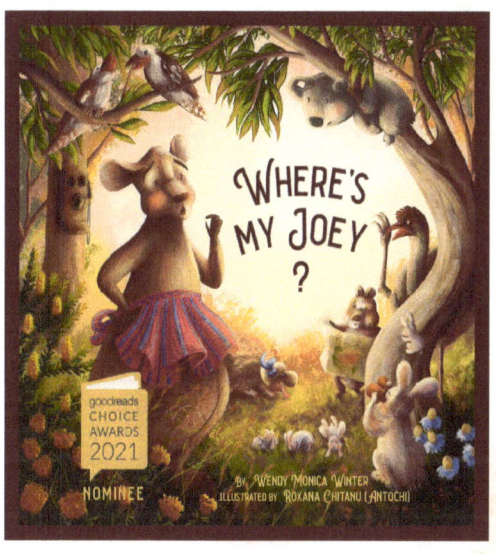

AND THE *WHERE'S MY JOEY?* COLORING BOOK

www.ingramcontent.com/pod-product-compliance
Lightning Source LLC
Chambersburg PA
CBHW042316280426
43673CB00080B/367